THE SCHOLASTIC
Big Book
of
Word Walls

100 Fresh & Fun Word Walls,
Easy Games, Activities, and Teaching Tips to
Help Kids Build Key Reading, Writing,
Spelling Skills and More!

by Mary Beth Spann

SCHOLASTIC
PROFESSIONAL BOOKS

NEW YORK • TORONTO • LONDON • AUCKLAND • SYDNEY
MEXICO CITY • NEW DELHI • HONG KONG • BUENOS AIRES

Dedication

To my dear husband, Frank, and to our children, Francesca and James.
There are no words in the world to tell you how much I love you all.
—MBS

Cover design by Josué Castilleja
Cover art by Vincent Ceci
Interior design by Solutions by Design, Inc.
Interior illustration by James Graham Hale

ISBN 0-439-16519-9

Contents

butterfly

heart

star

leaf

fish

ball

flower

butterfly

heart

star

leaf

fish

ball

flower

ACKNOWLEDGMENTS

With deepest gratitude to the following talented and caring teachers who generously contributed their creative ideas to this publication. Without you, this book would not have been possible. *

Nancy Aiello

Marilyn Barton

Tiffany Becher

Eleanor C. Berg

Beverly Brett

Lori Bross

Pauletta Brown

Virginia Browne

Holly Canham

Amy Cantrell

Sharon Clark

Jeanne Crider

Beth Curasco

Erin Sloan Darlage

Vanessa Davis

Valerie Delos Santos-Duarte

Deirdre DeWald

Julie DiDonna

Ann Marie Dingler

Stacey Dowling

Rudy Fuentes

Anne Gambrel

Katherine Garvey

Kristen Geller

Bill Gibbons

Candace Gibbons

Lynn Glatt

Lecia Greenway

Cori Healey

Nancy Hill

Lori Horner

Laura Komos

Christina Lackey

Judith Laz

Cheryl Lenhart

Carolyn D. Lewis

Carolyn Longbotham

Maureen Madigan

Lisa McQuinn

Elaine L. Modlo

Joshua Moore

Hope Naber

Kathy M. Nelson

Tom Nixon

Denise O'Leary

Lisa O'Rourke

Michelle Pearson

Lesley Pike

April Potter

Tracey Ramsey

Heather Ribaric

Denise Ross

Angela Shelley

Kristin Schlosser

Angela Sahr

Nancy Sharoff

Louise Skinner

Lori Smith Rios

Tracie Soderstrom

Sharlotte Spence

Bonnie Suchart

Tamesha Sumpter

Gail Tanner

Barbara Tessler

Debby Todd

Rachel Walmer

Sue Walter

Karen Watson

Melissa Williams

Valerie Williams

Liz Willis

Stacy Winters

Barbara Zelechoski

* Every effort has been made to contact contributors in order to confirm names for inclusion in this list. Our sincere apologies if any names were inadvertently omitted.

About This Book

Welcome to *The Scholastic Big Book of Word Walls*! This book is overflowing with outstanding Word Wall ideas, how-to's for developing stimulating models and designs, easy construction tips, strategies for use, and management secrets, plus suggestions for keeping Word Walls fresh and fun all year long. And the best part is that these ideas really *work* because we collected them from talented and creative teachers just like you—teachers who use Word Walls every day with their class! In each section, you'll find ways to begin putting Word Walls into action with your class today:

Getting Started

In this section, you'll find supply lists, management tips, and ideas for different types of Word Wall formats.

Basic Word Walls

Here you'll find step-by-step instructions for the most common types of Word Walls, such as the ABC Word Wall, the Chunking Word Wall, the Name Word Wall, and the 100th Day of School Word Wall.

Space-Savers

If you're short on wall surface, these ideas will "fit right in" with your plans!

Thematic Word Walls

In this section, you'll find themed Word Walls that integrate literacy into all areas of your curriculum. Reproducible templates help children create beautiful displays.

Word Wall Games & Activities

Turn to this section and beyond for almost 50 fresh and fun ways to get children involved with the Word Walls around them!

butterfly

heart

star

leaf

fish

ball

flower

What Is a Word Wall?

A Word Wall is a display of words targeted for word study. It is a visual reference point, a place in the classroom for the teacher and children to collect, analyze, organize and store words encountered together during reading, writing and oral language experiences. Word Walls can be developed for different reasons and to target different skills—but usually, with the teacher's guidance and collaboration, children help generate the words that will be displayed on the wall. The words themselves can be culled from many sources: poems, rhymes, chants, shared readings, environmental print, children's experiences, oral language, and so on. In this way, words are "harvested" from meaningful classroom contexts.

Read All About It

To learn more about Word Walls, read *Teaching Reading and Writing With Word Walls* by Janiel M. Wagstaff (Scholastic, 1999).

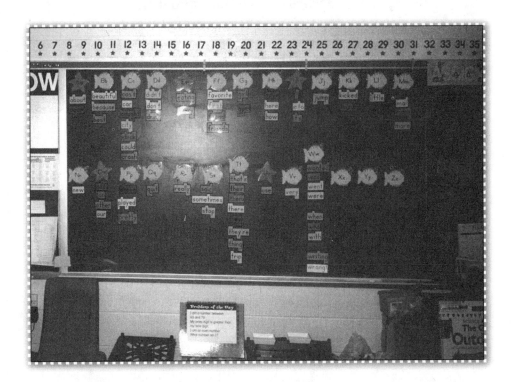

The Basics and Beyond

Ideally, a primary classroom would have a large bulletin board for displaying an ABC Word Wall, complete with word cards placed under the appropriate letters (see page 20). Many teachers find that a Chunking (or "Word Family") Word Wall, which has words chosen for the common spelling patterns or word families they represent also deserves classroom wall space (see page 27). While teachers across the country do build these basic models, many regard these Word Walls as springboards for other innovative and unique Word Wall arrangements and designs.

There are many reasons you might create a new or different type of Word Wall. Sometimes a novel Word Wall is called for because classroom space is a challenge. After all, not every classroom has a large, easy-to-access bulletin board just right for displaying a Word Wall! Some special-area teachers, for example, work outside the parameters of the ordinary classroom, storing supplies on carts to create "classrooms on wheels." Such "teachers on-the-go" might want to find a way to make portable Word Walls they can bring to the children.

Then, too, many teachers find they enjoy creative, alternative ways to introduce and display words before transferring them to the traditional Word Wall. Others develop different Word Walls to address specific learning goals (for example, for decoding purposes, or to display thematic or content-related vocabulary). Teachers also develop Word Walls that appeal to the specific needs and interests of their students, from pre-kindergarten through the upper elementary grades and beyond.

butterfly

heart

star

leaf

fish

ball

flower

If you are a Word Wall beginner, you may feel most comfortable starting out with a basic ABC Word Wall or a Chunking Word Wall. As you grow more confident with Word Walls, you'll be ready to manage multiple Word Wall designs. In addition to your main Word Wall model, perhaps you will include additional Word Walls designed to address particular vocabulary themes, word skills, or spelling patterns. You'll probably want your main Word Wall to stay up all year long, and display other models, such as holiday and seasonal Word Walls, for a short time only.

This book will introduce you to a host of ideas that teachers have developed in their classrooms. No matter what your needs or teaching situation, this book will show you Word Wall models that can work for you. Use this book to have fun exploring and experimenting with all sorts of Word Wall possibilities!

Tell children your ABC Word Wall is like a "Giant's Dictionary." Allow them direct access to the Word Wall so they may copy the words they need or check to see that they have spelled words correctly. Removable Word Wall cards allow children to take individual words back to their work area.

Why Use Word Walls?

> Word Walls are worth any effort you put into making, maintaining and using them with children. Here's why:

❄ **Word Walls elevate words to a starring role** in your classroom, sending children the message that reading and writing are important.

❄ **Word Walls are interactive tools** that invite children to actively participate in the process of analyzing, using, and manipulating words.

❄ **Word Walls give children ownership** over their learning.

❄ **Word Wall words are culled from authentic language experiences**; therefore, children see words in a meaningful context.

❄ **Word Walls encourage children to become independent** readers and writers.

❄ **Word Walls help you set visual, concrete learning goals** for each child.

❄ **Word Walls allow children to self-assess**—to recognize their own growing bank of word knowledge and mastery.

butterfly

heart

star

leaf

fish

ball

flower

Getting Started

Welcome to the wonderful world of Word Walls! Ease yourself and your students into working with Word Walls with these easy tips and models.

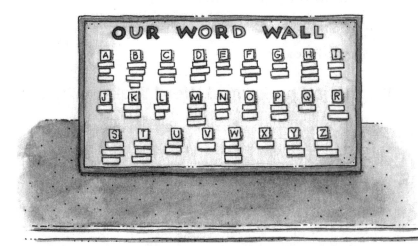

butterfly

heart

star

leaf

fish

ball

flower

Word Wall Supplies

What you'll need to begin your Word Wall depends on its design and the space available. However, some basic Word Wall designs are described below. Luckily, you probably have most of the basic necessities on hand:

Bulletin Board Word Walls

- ✿ craft paper
- ✿ borders
- ✿ staples or pushpins
- ✿ paper or index cards
- ✿ markers
- ✿ scissors

Pocket Chart Word Walls

- ✿ commercially made pocket chart
- ✿ sentence strip cards or index cards
- ✿ markers
- ✿ scissors

Chalkboard Word Walls

- ✿ water-soluble chalkboard markers
- ✿ chalk
- ✿ yardstick

Magnetic Chalkboard Word Walls

- ✿ water-soluble chalkboard markers
- ✿ self-sticking magnetic strips
- ✿ index cards or sentence strips
- ✿ markers
- ✿ scissors

Additional Word Wall models presented throughout the book almost always require similar classroom supplies. If space is an issue for you, read the ideas in "Space Savers" (pages 31-50)

butterfly

heart

star

leaf

fish

ball

flower

Management Tips

❋ Whenever possible, build Word Wall displays at children's eye level and within their reach. Even if you design your Word Wall so that the word cards are not removable, children should be able to go to the Word Wall and copy words directly into their writing.

❋ As your Word Wall fills up, transfer words children have mastered to a secondary display, perhaps located over a chalkboard or behind a door.

❋ Each week, print out a list of the words featured on the Word Wall (you can use different-colored ink or an asterisk to highlight any new words that have been added to the Wall). Make copies of the list and give to children to store in their individual Word Wall pocket folders, looseleaf folders, or writing folders.

❋ Assign the job of "Word Wall Keeper" as one of the responsibilities on your class job chart. The Keeper is responsible for placing new words on the wall and making sure word cards are replaced on the wall.

Class Job Chart

Attendance Taker: Francesca
Lunch Monitor: Katie
Line Leader: Ellen
Craft Clean-up: James Sinead
Word Wall Keeper: Curtis

butterfly
heart
star
leaf
fish
ball
flower

butterfly

heart

star

leaf

fish

ball

flower

✿ Educate parents about the importance Word Walls play in your program and enlist their help through volunteering during writing time. Walk parent volunteers through the process of helping children use your Word Wall system.

✿ Remember: Frequency is key to working with Word Walls. Teachers who are most successful with Word Walls suggest visiting the Word Wall at least once a week, if not every day. Make Word Wall visits a habit, even if for a few minutes at a time. Don't worry that your Word Wall experiences will become monotonous — this book is filled with ideas for keeping Word Walls fresh and fun-filled all year long!

✿ If possible, set aside an uncluttered, accessible area in the classroom for your Word Wall display. It's ideal if your Word Wall area includes space for the whole class to gather as closely as possible so that introducing and reviewing words can be a whole-group activity.

Word Wall Models

Here are some different formats to consider as you think about creating your Word Wall:

Write-On/Wipe-Off Word Wall Charts

Laminate large pieces of white chart paper (you might decorate the borders first) and use a dry erase marker to write words onto them (you can use a magnetic spring clip to display charts on a magnetic chalk board). You might also punch holes at the top of each chart to hang a collection of charts from a chart holder. When you accumulate a number of charts featuring different collections of words, simply flip back and forth among charts as needed. As children master words (or as you wish to generate new words with a different group of children), simply erase old words and replace.

Color-Coded Word Walls

Use colored index cards to help color-code your Word Wall. For example, if setting up a "Parts of Speech" Word Wall, use red cards for nouns, green for verbs, and blue for adjectives. You can also feature words from different curriculum areas (for example, orange for language arts, green for math). With this strategy, you can still arrange cards in alphabetical order. It's a good idea to post a color key for children to refer to.

Big, Bold Words

Use a computer and printer to print Word Wall words in 72-point font that children can easily read from a distance. As children become more proficient readers, you might try printing the same words in several different styles so children become used to reading words in a variety of fonts.

Double Duty Word Cards

As you create cards for use on your Word Wall, make a duplicate set for children to manipulate in learning center games and activities. Then, send updated word lists home to families and encourage them to record the words on index cards with their children at home.

Shapely Word Wall Cards

Instead of using ordinary index cards or sentence strips for Word Wall words, try cutting out fun-shaped word cards. These work especially well when recording thematic word collections, such as penguin shapes for a Penguin Word Wall. The shapes can also be used to record words related to a particular alphabet letter, such as fish shapes for a "Words Beginning with Ff" Word Wall. To save time, you might purchase pre-cut shape cards or small shaped note pads. Record words on these shapes, then laminate for future use.

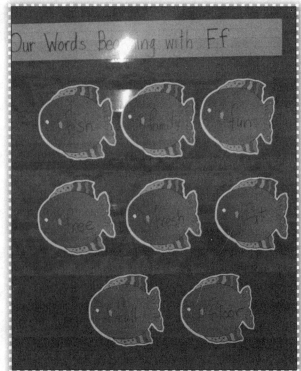

Sticky Notes Word Wall

After recording words on your Word Wall, write the same words on removable self-sticking notes. Have children match the notes to the permanent word display, then press them in place. The notes can be removed for writing games and activities (children can take the notes down, stick them on their shirts, and arrange themselves to create silly sentences). Replace when the stickiness wears off the originals.

3D Word Wall

Have children use art supplies or building blocks to construct a building, sculpture or other structure. Talk about the structure—the materials children used, the shapes they notice, and so on—and use this discussion to generate a list of words to attach directly to it. You might photograph children's buildings and place the photos in an album along with the lists of words each one generated.

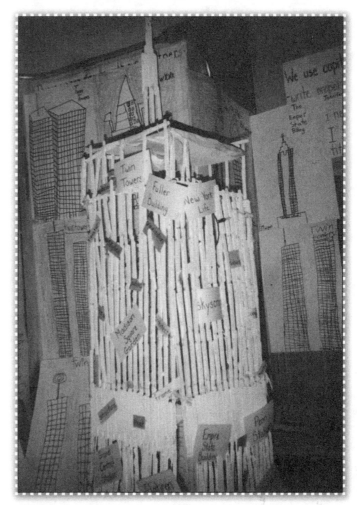

Children used wooden craft sticks to build this New York City Skyscraper Word Wall, then displayed names of area buildings and landmarks.

Basic Word Walls

Here are some popular approaches to creating Word Walls—and ideas for putting them to work!

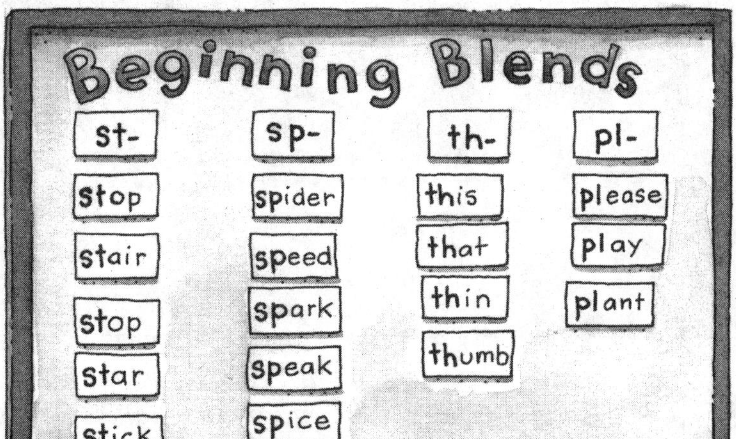

Beginning Blends

st-	sp-	th-	pl-
stop	spider	this	please
stair	speed	that	play
stop	spark	thin	plant
star	speak	thumb	
stick	spice		

butterfly

heart

star

leaf

fish

ball

flower

ABC Word Wall

> **Build children's understanding of initial sounds.**

1 For this popular Word Wall, cover a large bulletin board in craft paper.

2 Use a marker or border paper to divide the display in half, horizontally.

3 Section the display into 13 equal columns and label each of the resulting 26 sections with one letter of the alphabet.

4 Use index cards to record words you wish to display. Cull words from literature selections, class discussions and studies, or children's own writing.

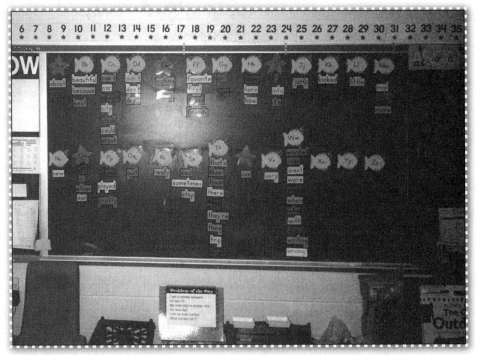

An ABC Word Wall displayed on a magnetic chalkboard. The words stick to the display with the help of a magnetic strip glued to the back of each card.

Teacher Tip

Use a contrasting color marker to outline the shape of each printed word or to underline word family endings.

Phonetic Features Word Wall

Showcase words that share a particular feature.

1 Try a phonetically-based Word Wall display to focus children's attention on patterns. Address one or more of the following: beginning consonants, short or long vowels, consonant blends, beginning and ending blends, rhyming words, and homophones.

2 To help children focus on these features, you might have them use markers to outline or underline the letter or letters that make up the pattern in each word.

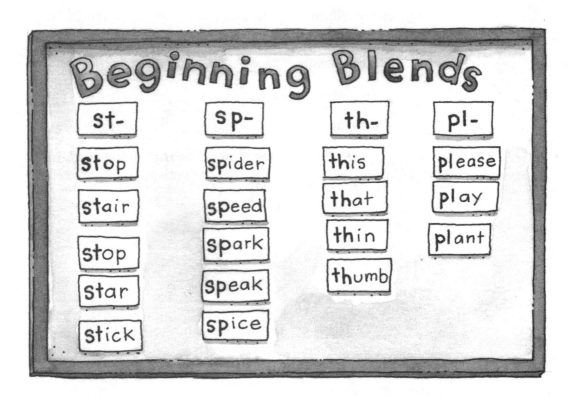

Beginning Blends

st-	sp-	th-	pl-
stop	spider	this	please
stair	speed	that	play
stop	spark	thin	plant
star	speak	thumb	
stick	spice		

Name Word Wall

> **Create a beginning-of-the-year, back-to-school Word Wall that features each child's first name.**

1 Make black and white photocopies of the children's school photos (you might use school records or ask their previous teacher) and glue each child's photo to an index card. Write their names on the cards.

2 Display these name cards at children's eye level on background shapes, such as paper dolls, colorful balloons, or birthday cakes (labeled with each child's birthday) cut from craft paper.

3 After children are familiar with the name cards, transfer them to a pocket chart, where children can:

- ❈ arrange the names in alphabetical order
- ❈ clap the syllables in each name
- ❈ locate names containing short or long vowel sounds
- ❈ locate names containing diphthongs or letter blends
- ❈ play name games (such as guessing which name is missing)

Teacher Tip

Children's name cards may eventually be added to a basic ABC Word Wall (see page 20). Consider adding other names to your collection, including those of faculty members, school workers, and classroom visitors.

Photo Word Wall

This Word Wall model is a variation of the Name Word Wall (page 22).

1. Begin by setting up an ABC Word Wall (see page 20) to display children's first names and photos.

2. Over time, take photos of classroom happenings, events, and field trips to add to your Word Wall, along with descriptive labels.

3. Ask children to contribute additional photos from home to illustrate any letter or sound you wish to target.

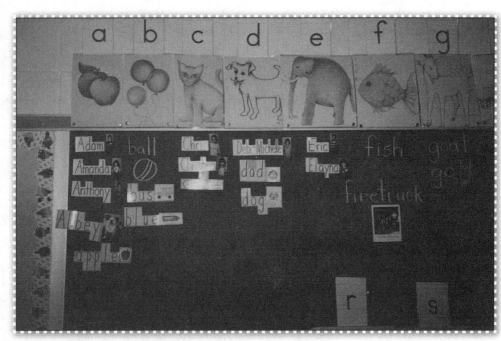

This Photo Word Wall features photos of children labeled with their first names; later in the year, last names will be added.

Parts of Speech Word Wall

> **Feature a collection of one word type.**

 Choose a specific word type you wish to target.

 Write down individual words on index cards. You might include nouns, pronouns, verbs, adjectives, adverbs, prepositions, conjunctions, synonyms, antonyms, homophones, contractions or interjections.

 Before displaying a new Word Wall, record each word collection on chart paper for future use.

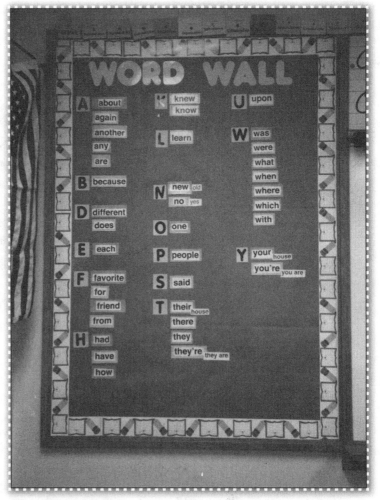

This Word Wall features homophones as well as difficult-to-decode high frequency words.

100th Day of School Word Wall

> **Begin this Word Wall on the first day of school, then add to it daily until the 100th Day!**

1 Cover a large bulletin board with craft paper. Number and label brightly colored pieces of paper or index cards with the words you wish to mount on the wall.

2 Add one word every day. Periodically, try to use the words in a cumulative story: You begin the story, and each child adds a sentence using a Word Wall word.

3 You might continue adding words to this wall until the last day of school. Alternatively, you can initiate this Word Wall any time during the school year for any length of time.

Variation

Feature the words (placing one word a day on the Wall) for each of the numerals from one to one hundred.

 butterfly

 heart

 star

leaf

fish

ball

flower

Cross-Curricular Word Wall

> **Develop Word Walls that feature vocabulary related to a specific area of your curriculum.**

1 You can set up Word Walls to address math terms and symbols, geography terms and definitions, and science or social studies vocabulary.

2 Post corresponding definitions next to each term. You can also attach cards to the display using a tape "hinge" so children can lift up the cards to reveal definitions printed on the space beneath.

Word Family Word Wall

> A Word Family, or Chunking, Word Wall can help children focus on spelling patterns and word-family endings.

This model is similar to the ABC Word Wall described on page 20, but, instead of arranging word cards in alphabetical order, words are chosen and grouped according to their word-family ending features (phonograms). The most common phonograms are listed here (see left).

You may want your wall to feature only some of these word families at one time. You can use this same Word Wall model to feature prefixes and suffixes.

-ack	-ay	-ip
-ail	-eat	-ir
-ain	-ell	-ock
-ake	-est	-oke
-ale	-ice	-or
-ame	-ick	-ore
-an	-ide	-op
-ank	-ight	-uck
-ap	-ill	-ug
-ash	-in	-ump
-at	-ine	-unk
-ate	-ing	
-aw	-ink	

One set of Word Family cards displayed in a pocket chart.

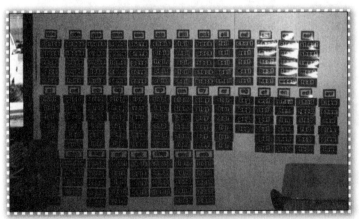

A typical Word Family Word Wall.

Environmental Print Display

This easy-to-create Word Wall reflects children's interests, while expanding their print awareness.

1 Enlist children's help in clipping and collecting printed logos from packaging, magazines, and advertisements.

2 Title your Word Wall "Look What We Can Read!" and add to it over time, reviewing the words frequently.

3 Have children manipulate the words by inviting them to arrange or group them in different ways, such as alphabetically, according to number of syllables, or thematically (toy words, food words).

Teacher Tip

Typical logos might include those from fast food restaurants, popular toys, children's television shows and movies, favorite brand-name foods, and clothing stores.

Literature Word Wall

> **Display words culled from a book or story you are currently reading in class.**

1 As you read a story or book, create word cards and have children glue them onto pieces of oaktag, adding illustrations to create a vocabulary collage.

2 Meanwhile, record each set of words on a separate piece of chart paper marked with the title of that story or book.

3 Children might copy the words into alphabetized "Vocabulary Notebooks" they maintain all year long.

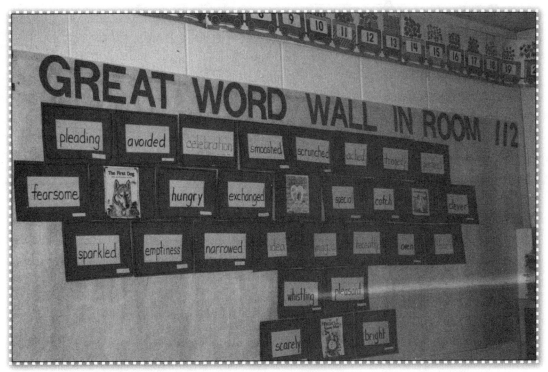

This "Great Word Wall" features illustrations and words from shared literature selections. Illustrations and word cards are mounted on pieces of black construction paper outlined with black marker so each one resembles a block in the wall.

butterfly

heart

star

leaf

fish

ball

flower

Concept Word Wall

Help children focus on beginning letters while building concept-related vocabulary.

1 Decide on a target concept you wish to address, such as size, color, shape, feelings, or places.

2 Along the top of your Word Wall display, post a title card for the category (SIZE WORDS, COLOR WORDS, and so on), with letters A to Z printed below.

3 Children can then generate words for each letter.

ALPHABET ZOO

A	nteater, armadillo, ant	F	rog	L	ynx, lion	R	obin	X	x-ray fish
B	ee, bear	G	oat, gorilla	M	onkey	S	nake shark	Y	ak
C	at, coyote	H	yena	N	ewt	T	urtle	
D	og, dear	I	guana	O	ctopus	U	mbrella bird	Z	ebra
E	lephant	J	aguar jackal	P	anda praying mantis	V	iper	
		K	oala	Q	uail	W	alrus wombat	

Teacher Tip

Concept-based alphabet books can provide inspiration for these combination Concept/ABC Word Walls.

butterfly

heart

star

leaf

fish

ball

flower

Space-Savers

Word Walls don't have to stay on the wall! If you're short on wall surface, try these space-saving techniques.

Portable File Folder Word Wall

Build children's vocabularies with these easy-to-make-and-store Word Walls.

 You'll need a supply of file folders (one or more per child) and a free-standing folder holder. Label the outside front and tab of each folder with the featured theme or target skill ("Our Farm Words," "Words Ending in -<u>ing</u>," and so on).

Teacher Tip

These file folders work especially well for content area vocabulary words. You can help each child personalize his or her own collection of file folder Word Walls.

Children can decorate the front of their files with drawings, stickers or glued-on pictures. Then, use the inside of each folder to record themed words. You can generate the words on a large piece of chart paper first, then have children transfer the list to a folder.

Place the folders into a folder holder and place the holder in your writing center for children to access as needed.

Read All About It

To learn more about thematic file folder Word Walls, read *Portable File Folder Word Walls* by Mary Beth Spann (Scholastic, 1999).

A child's own portable file folder Word Wall. Note child-decorated and labeled folder front, plus word review activity on back.

butterfly

heart

star

leaf

fish

ball

flower

Word Wall Floor Show

> **This Word Wall needs no wall space at all!**

1 Print your target words on stone-shaped cards cut from gray construction paper.

2 Laminate the cards for durability, then spread them on the floor away from highly-trafficked areas.

3 Children can sort, group, and arrange the cards in a variety of ways. You can play stepping-stone reading games in which children hop on one foot to words you read aloud, or arrange words (for instance, those belonging to a particular word family, or theme) in a path so children can read the words as they walk along.

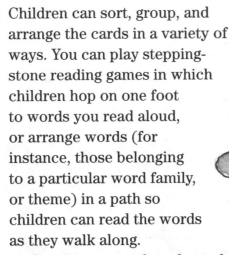

Or, arrange word cards on the floor in a straight line. Use carpet tape (which will not leave sticky residue on carpet) to adhere the cards to the floor. Offer each child a turn to leap-frog from one word to the next as they read each word.

Variation

Play Twister! Cut out construction paper circles that match the colors and size of those shown on the Twister game mat, write words on them and use carpet tape to attach the cards to the mat. Use the game's spinner to direct players where to place hands and feet. To stay in the game, children read the words on the circles they touch.

Skinny Word Wall

Use any skinny vertical space in your classroom, including spaces you wouldn't ordinarily consider to be display spots. Even hall lockers can be put to use!

1. Use self-sticking Velcro strips and index cards to turn space into a vertical Word Wall. Place a strip on one side of each card and the other strip on the wall surface.

2. Write words on the cards and arrange them in the grouping of your choice.

3. Periodically strip away all cards and begin with a new set of word cards.

Velcro strips turn unused lockers into a hallway Word Wall.

Vocabulary Vine

Children will be delighted as words creep into every available classroom nook and cranny—and even dangle from the ceiling.

1 Use twisted lengths of green crepe paper or yarn to create a Word Wall vine that grows all over your classroom! With strong tape, attach large green paper leaves printed with words.

2 Challenge children to try reading from beginning to end of the vine.

Teacher Tip

By laminating the leaves and using dry-erase marker, you can easily erase the words. You can also include other colors or decorations. In the fall, display words on colored leaves; in winter add some snowflakes; in spring, shamrocks or flower shapes.

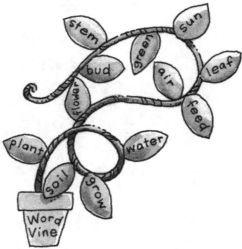

Bilingual Word Wall

Build second-language skills.

If you want to display words in both English and a second language, but lack the space for more than one Word Wall, try using different-colored index cards. Assign one color to each language.

Flannel Board Fun

Use a flannel board for a Word Wall display.

1 Laminate a stack of index cards and glue a piece of Velcro, felt, or rough sandpaper to the back of each one.

2 Use a dry-erase marker to record a word on each card. Attach the cards to a flannel board.

3 To write new words, simply wipe clean.

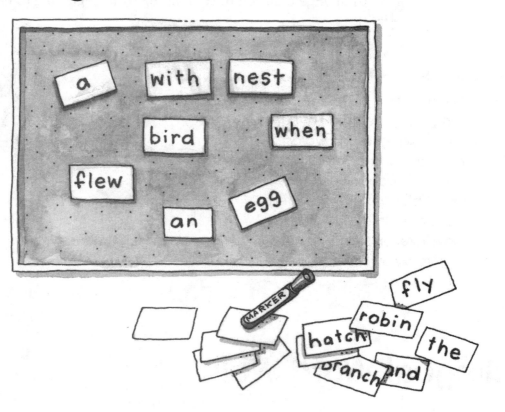

Outdoor Word Walls

For a change of pace, get permission to use sidewalk chalk to write words on the playground blacktop or concrete.

1 Children can draw a hopscotch grid on the ground and record Word Wall words in the different squares.

2 Players take turns throwing a pebble on one word at a time and hopping over that word.

3 On the way back to HOME, the player picks up the pebble and correctly reads the word.

Variation

You can also use sidewalk chalk to draw a simple ladder on the ground and write one word on each rung. To "climb" the ladder, children read and spell each word.

 star

 leaf

 fish

File Folder Word Wall Offices

To make your Word Wall visible to all children (no matter what your room's arrangement!), have each child make an "office" for his or her desk.

1 Place two file folders side by side, with ends overlapping.

2 Use clear packing tape to attach these overlapping ends, creating one long side (the "front" of the office) and two short sides (the "sides" of the office).

3 Invite children to decorate their offices. On the inside, children write Word Wall words. You might personalize a word list for each child, or have children write synonyms, adjectives, action verbs, a self-editing checklist, or anything else they need references for.

Teacher Tip

These offices can be stored flat when not in use, and popped open any time. They also provide children with privacy for writing, journaling, or reading.

Magnetic Chalkboard

A magnetic chalkboard is an easy-to-use Word Wall display.

1 Write words on index cards. Place self-sticking magnetic strips on the back of the cards so that they can be moved around and taken off a magnetic chalkboard easily.

2 When children need to refer to a word when writing, they can easily remove the cards from the magnetic Word Wall, then place them back on the board when finished.

Chart Pictionaries

Instead of relying on traditional Word Walls, try creating seasonal or thematic "pictionaries."

1 On pieces of oaktag or chart paper, generate word lists (based upon a certain area of study) with the group.

2 Invite each child to illustrate one word on a large index card and label their picture.

3 Display the pictures together on a chart holder or chalk tray, or suspended from the ceiling with wire.

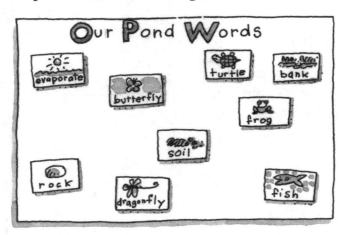

File Cabinet Word Wall

The side of a metal file cabinet can double as a Word Wall.

 Make your own word cards by laminating blank index cards or sentence strips, sticking a self-adhesive magnetic piece to the back of each, and then using a wipe-off marker to record words.

 Children can easily manipulate these magnetic words on the side surface of a metal cabinet. They can put the words in alphabetical order, make sentences, group according to spelling patterns, and so on.

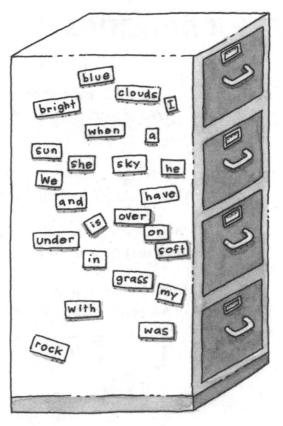

Variation

Use a large metal cookie sheet and words from magnetic poetry kits.

butterfly

heart

star

leaf

fish

ball

flower

High Wire Word Walls

When space is really at a premium, you can dangle Word Walls from ceiling wires, hanging the words low enough for children to see them.

Here are some to try:

❁ Laundry Day Word Wall

Cut and label large sheets of paper into "laundry" shapes and label each with a letter of the alphabet. Use each shape to list other words beginning with the same alphabet letter (letters and words should be printed on both sides of the shape so all children can read them). Use clothespins to hang these shapes from ceiling wire or clothesline so they resemble wash drying on the line!

❀ Hanging Banner Word Wall

Use masking tape to cover the hook of a wire clothes hanger. Cut a length of craft paper as wide as the coat hanger, and use the paper to record related words (words beginning with the same letter, words belonging to the same word family, thematic words, and so on). Then, tape the banner to the coat hanger, making certain the list is hung low enough for children to read. (Store these lists for review or future use.)

❀ Adding Machine Tape Word Wall

Thread a pipe cleaner through a roll of adding machine tape (available in stationary supply stores) and attach to ceiling wire. The paper can be unspooled bit by bit to record and display words children generate over time, such as a list of adjectives. Tape a penny to the free end of the tape so it won't curl.

Desktop Dictionary Word Wall

Make a desktop "dictionary" for quick reference.

1 Purchase an alphabetized, "turnable" file box, such as those made by Rolodex.

2 Write words on the cards and help children arrange them in alphabetical order.

3 Children can turn the knob or flip through the tabs to locate words!

Teacher Tip

Even if you have a traditional Word Wall display, this is a great way to make the words accessible to children. You can also take words off your Word Wall and know they are still available to children in the file box. To practice alphabetizing, children might remove the cards, shuffle them, and replace them in the correct order.

butterfly

heart

star

leaf

fish

ball

flower

Read Around the Room

Label everything in your classroom—from desks and chairs to the floor and ceiling!

1. Have children use index cards to label objects all over the room: clock, door, map, and so on.

2. Focus on activities that expose children to the words in the room. To promote directionality and mapping skills, have children locate words in relation to nearby objects: above, below, next to, beneath, east of, west of, and so on.

Canned Word Wall

 Record words on wooden craft sticks and place into a covered juice can with the "contents" clearly labeled. For instance, a can labeled "Plants" would have sticks with words such as *roots*, *cultivate*, and so on. Craft sticks are more durable than index cards, and children love to manipulate them!

 Play word games, such as Pick-Up-Stick-Words, in which you dump all the sticks out in a heap and have children take turns trying to read and remove one word at a time without disturbing the others. Chidren might also alphabetize all the words in the can.

Colored Chalk Word Wall

> **In addition to automatically grouping the words visually for children, colored chalks help keep a display bright.**

1 On a chalkboard, use different colors of chalk to record different parts of speech or groups of words with different phonetic features.

2 When you are ready to erase a group of words, use the same-colored marker to print them on index cards and store in a box in the writing center.

Variation

Children can create the wall themselves. Give them one word at a time and challenge them to determine which color to use.

butterfly

heart

star

leaf

fish

ball

flower

Dry-Erase Marker Word Wall

> **Turn a black or green magnetic chalkboard into an ABC Word Wall.**

1 Use a marker made specifically for dry-erase boards (such as Bright Stick™) to divide your board into columns wide enough to hold word cards (the marker lines will not wipe off; however, they will erase when washed with water).

2 Write each letter of the alphabet, upper and lower case, on an index card. Attach a magnet to the back of each card and arrange cards alphabetically on the board.

3 Record words on sentence strips or index cards. Place a self-sticking magnetic strip on the back of each card and display under the corresponding letter.

Teacher Tip

You can also use colored chalks to record words directly on the Word Wall. When you are ready to erase and replace words, the dry erase marker lines will remain.

Vertical chalkboard marker lines help divide this magnetic chalkboard into columns.

Over the Top Word Wall

Word Walls are best located so children can access them—but when you're short on display space, sometimes the only way to go is up!

 Spaces above chalkboards and bulletin boards can be used as Word Wall space. Make letters large so children can read them from a distance.

 Mat words on contrasting color background paper and post. (You might provide children with a more accessible version of the same words, such as lists posted inside file folders.)

This ABC Word Wall, displayed above the chalkboard, features words matted on different colored pieces of construction paper.

butterfly

heart

star

leaf

fish

ball

flower

Month-by-Month Chart Stand

> **Focus on a new set of words each month.**

1 Laminate 10 large pieces of white chart paper and use each to record a set of words for one month of the school year.

2 During lessons, encourage children to suggest words for the Word Wall. Record the words with dry-erase marker.

3 Display the "words of the month" on a chart stand. From time to time, review all the words you have learned together.

butterfly

heart

star

leaf

fish

ball

flower

Big Shapes Word Wall

1 Cut out large shapes related to a theme you are studying and record words directly on the shapes. For example, use a ladybug shape to record words related to insect study, or a large paper snowman to record winter words.

2 Display shapes around the classroom. Children can scan the room to locate the shape that features the word they are looking for.

Teacher Tip

Decorate your shapes with just enough detail so children recognize each shape, but not so much detail that it is visually distracting.

SNOW!

snowman
snowflake
snowsuit
snowball
snowshoes
snowstorm
snow angels

butterfly

heart

star

leaf

fish

ball

flower

Thematic Word Walls

Word Walls can be themed for any holiday, occasion, or curriculum unit!

butterfly

heart

star

leaf

fish

ball

flower

Back-to-School Word Wall

Have this Word Wall display ready on the first day of school as a "welcoming" introduction.

1 Cover a bulletin board with light blue craft paper to resemble the sky. Cut out a simple schoolhouse shape from red craft paper and place this in the center of the display. Use marker to add a ground line.

2 Glue a photo of your face to a large paper doll shape you've cut from paper and decorated with markers to look like you!

3 Fold an additional length of craft paper accordion style and cut a string of paper dolls so that you have one doll per child.

4 Label index cards with each child's name and post. When children arrive, have them "sign into" class by drawing a face and clothing on their doll's shape.

Teacher Tip

Add cloud shapes with school-related words (school, reading, library, books, math, music, computer, recess) to your display. Also, when you are ready to dismantle the Word Wall, you can use the name cards as the beginning of your basic ABC Word Wall.

Family Tree Word Wall

> **Grow a word tree full of family-related vocabulary.**

1 To "grow" a family tree Word Wall, first cut out a large tree trunk shape from brown craft paper. Use a black marker to add bark and "knotty" lines and staple to a bulletin board.

2 Cut out leaf-shaped word cards (copy page 54 onto colored paper).

3 Label each leaf with a family word such as *brother, sister, aunt, cousin, grandmother, grandfather, niece.*

4 Each time you add a new leaf to your tree, discuss the meaning and significance of that word. You might also use the leaves to record Autumn words.

Variation

Provide each child with a number of paper leaves to take home. Have children draw or mount pictures of relatives on the leaves, then label with the name and relationship of that relative to the child.

butterfly

heart

star

leaf

fish

ball

flower

Leaf Template

Friendship Word Wall

1. Have children trace and cut out a supply of hand shapes.

2. Then, help them use the shapes to record friendship-related words to use on a Friendship Word Wall or a Peacemaker Word Wall.

3. The hand shapes may be displayed together in the shape of a friendship heart, or stretch around the room as a border that surrounds children with words.

butterfly

heart

star

leaf

fish

ball

flower

Weather Window Word Wall

Build seasonal vocabulary with weather symbols.

1 Cover a large bulletin board with sky-blue paper. Use a wide-tipped black marker to divide the wall into fourths, representing four window panes.

2 Add a large yellow sun in the center of the upper right pane, a white snowflake in the upper left pane, an umbrella in the lower left pane and a leaf in the lower right pane.

3 Then, copy page 57 onto white paper so each child can decorate and record a summer weather word to post near the sun, a winter word around the snowflake, a spring word around the umbrella and an autumn word around the leaf.

SEASONAL WORD LIST			
spring	**summer**	**fall**	**winter**
flower	sun	leaves	December
grow	beach	colors	January
rain	June	crisp	snow
April	July	October	ice
mud	August	November	frost
birds	lotion		slippery
March	hot		freezing
	humid		chilly
			snowman

butterfly

heart

star

leaf

fish

ball

flower

Toy Word Wall

Use children's favorite things to build language skills.

1 Invite children to bring in toys (or pictures of toys) related to a topic you are exploring. For example, if you are learning about woodland animals, children might bring in stuffed animals or models.

2 Have children arrange these objects on a display desk or table, then help children use index cards to label each toy.

3 Later, add these words to your ABC Word Wall.

Feelings Word Wall

Help children use words to describe their feelings.

1 Make a list of "feeling" words with children, encouraging them to contribute words more precise than *sad*, *mad*, or *happy* (such as *delighted*, *calm*, or *grouchy*).

2 Give each child a paper plate and art supplies, and invite them to choose a feeling to illustrate on a "face."

3 Help them label their feeling and post their face on the Word Wall.

4 Let them add to the Word Wall as they discover new words for feelings.

Word Wall Mascot

Scour garage sales and flea markets for a large plush toy, then use it as a 3-D Word Wall mascot to introduce new words to your class.

1 Tape word cards directly to the toy. After reviewing each word with children, transfer the cards to your main Word Wall.

2 You can use a funny voice to make your mascot "talk" by tape recording a message from your mascot to the class! The message might invite children to locate particular word cards and then move them to a certain place on the Word Wall.

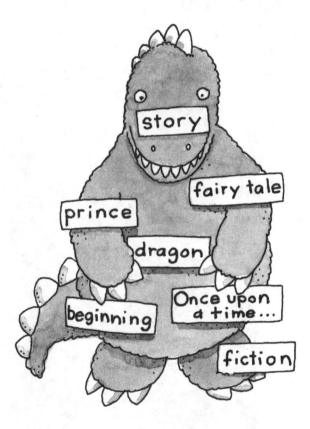

Bony Word Wall

Build vocabulary with a spooky, seasonal Word Wall.

1 Purchase a paper skeleton from a party supply store or card store.

2 Display the skeleton along with "bones" featuring Halloween words, or words related to body parts (copy page 61). Also, cut out a supply of speech balloons (also on page 61) and print each with a different target word.

3 Each day, place one balloon near the skeleton's mouth so it appears to be introducing a Word of the Day. At each day's end, have a child copy that word onto a bone and add that word to the Word Wall.

This Halloween time Word Wall includes words for body parts.

Thanksgiving Turkey Word Wall

Integrate literacy into your holiday observances.

1 Cut a round turkey body from brown craft paper. Cut a supply of individual feathers (copy page 63 onto different colors of paper).

2 On each feather, have children record a word related to the season or holiday. Use double-sided tape to attach the feathers to the turkey.

3 In addition, you can use a paper speech balloon to have the turkey announce a new Word of the Day. (See Bony Word Wall on page 60 for how-to's.)

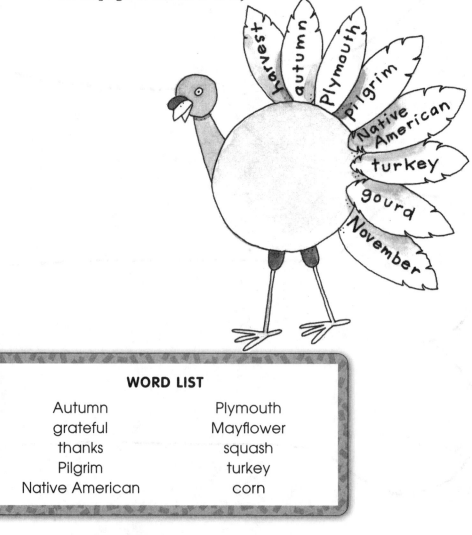

WORD LIST

Autumn	Plymouth
grateful	Mayflower
thanks	squash
Pilgrim	turkey
Native American	corn

butterfly

heart

star

leaf

fish

ball

flower

Feather Template

Penguin Rookery Word Wall

When studying Arctic penguins (or any winter-related subject), set up a Penguin Word Wall.

 Cover a bulletin board with light blue paper.

 Loosely crumple lengths of white paper (large "ice chunks") and staple these to the display.

3 Staple penguin shapes (copy page 65) onto the "ice" and use these shapes to record words related to your unit of study.

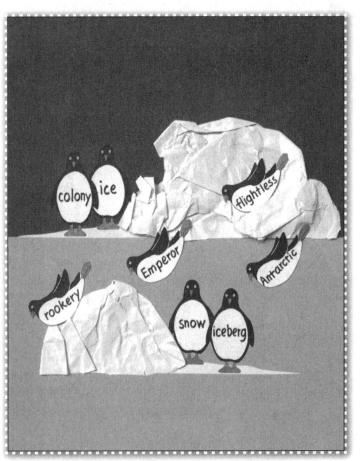

Penguin-related vocabulary is recorded on an icy Word Wall.

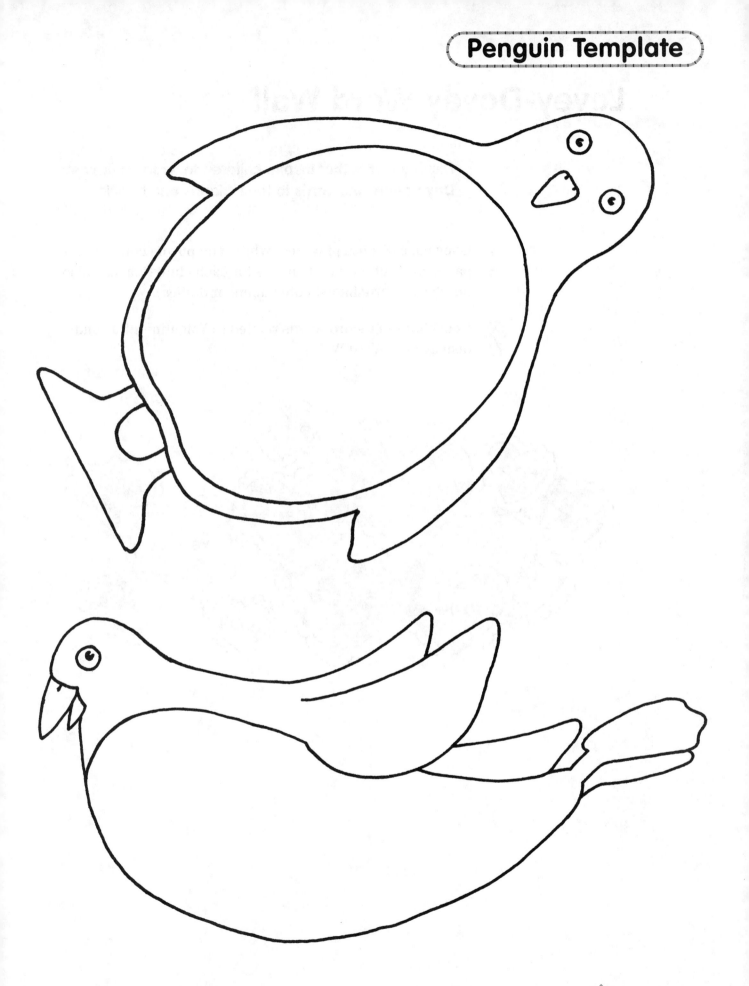

Lovey-Dovey Word Wall

Display words that inspire children to write Valentine's Day poems and cards to their friends and families.

 Copy page 67 onto pink, red, white, and purple construction paper, and cut out heart shapes for each child (you can also purchase heart-shaped note papers or doilies).

2 Help children record words related to Valentine's Day and display on a Word Wall.

butterfly

heart

star

leaf

fish

ball

flower

Butterfly Garden Word Wall

> **Bring spring inside while building vocabulary!**

1 Cover a bulletin board with light blue paper.

2 Copy page 69 and 70 onto colored paper and cut out the butterfly and flower shapes. Use them to record words related to a unit on butterflies, life cycles, or spring.

Teacher Tip

Short on wall space? Have the butterflies flutter up, around and over the doors, walls, and other displays in your classroom!

BUTTERFLY GARDEN WORD LIST

metamorphosis	larva
symmetry	eggs
Monarch	chrysalis
antennae	cocoon
colorful	nectar
caterpillar	life cycle
pupa	thorax

butterfly

heart

star

leaf

fish

ball

flower

Flower Template

Even More Thematic Word Walls

You can create Word Walls on almost any theme you wish. Here are some ideas for things to include on different Word Walls.

Baby Face Word Wall: children's baby pictures, baby-related words and first words (ask families to provide a list).

Safety Word Wall: shapes resembling traffic and road signs with safety words.

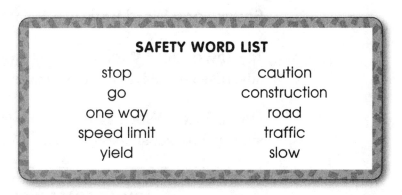

SAFETY WORD LIST	
stop	caution
go	construction
one way	road
speed limit	traffic
yield	slow

Harvest Word Wall: a large paper cornucopia with words printed on paper fruit and vegetable shapes (see page 74).

Apples or Pumpkins Word Wall: an apple tree with words printed on apple shapes, or a pumpkin patch with words on pumpkin shapes (also page 74).

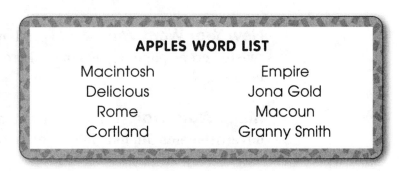

APPLES WORD LIST	
Macintosh	Empire
Delicious	Jona Gold
Rome	Macoun
Cortland	Granny Smith

butterfly

heart

star

leaf

fish

ball

flower

Doll House Word Wall: a large craft-paper house and yard shape divided into rooms with furniture and decorations cut from catalogs or from furniture store flyers. Pictures can be cut, glued, and labeled at each room.

DOLL HOUSE WORD LIST

bedroom	foyer	carpet
bathroom	ceiling	table
living room	wall	chair
kitchen	roof	bed
dining room	door	

Snack Food Word Wall: words cut from snack packages.

Toy Town Word Wall: names of toys cut from advertisements, flyers, and packages.

Outer Space Word Wall: space-related words on paper stars and rocket shapes (see page 75).

OUTER SPACE WORD LIST

star	planet
moon	Milky Way
orbit	light years
rocket	comet
astronaut	

New Year Word Wall: words printed on paper ribbon or twisted crepe paper against a background decorated with confetti.

Menu Word Wall: names of restaurants cut from advertisements. Include menus of favorite restaurants.

butterfly

heart

star

leaf

fish

ball

flower

Alliterative Pairs Word Wall: a display of alliterative terms.

Cooking Word Wall: cooking terms recorded on paper chef's hats, utensils, tools and recipes (see page 76).

COOKING WORD LIST

blend	ounce	sauté
mix	teaspoon	grill
whip	cup	chef
stir	bake	chop
measure	fry	whisk

Ant Farm Word Wall: a gigantic ant farm featuring ant- and insect-related words (see page 77). Also include words related to working together (*cooperate, leader, participate*) and ant movement (*crawl, line up, build*). You might cut an anthill shape from sandpaper.

Scrapbooking Word Wall: a thematic photo display, such as photos of monthly classroom events. Photos and labels can be placed in a scrapbook as new Scrapbook Word Walls are developed.

"Our Community" Word Wall: rectangle "buildings" cut from craft paper, each labeled with store names cut from magazines, newspapers or flyers. The "inside" of each store can be decorated and labeled with pictures of items for sale in that store. (Each child can design and label a store geared to his or her interests.) Children can create signs for various locations, such as library, skating rink, park, and so on.

butterfly

heart

star

leaf

fish

ball

flower

Harvest Template

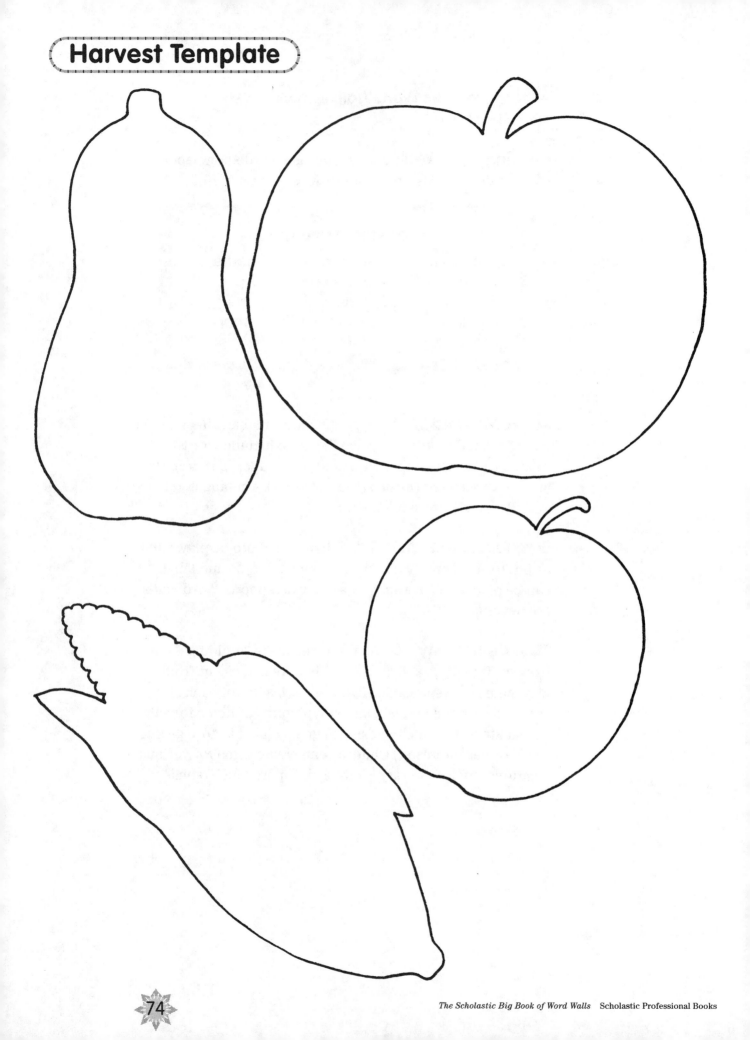

Cooking Template

Word Wall
Games & Activities

Engage children in Word Wall fun with games and activities that build listening, reading, writing, and spelling skills, and more.

butterfly

heart

star

leaf

fish

ball

flower

Timed Word Wall Test

1. After children have become familiar with the words on your Word Wall, and if they will respond positively to such a challenge, have them see how many words they can correctly read in one minute.

2. Repeat the exercise every few weeks throughout the school year, so each child can see improvement over time. You might enlist a parent volunteer to time each child's reading efforts.

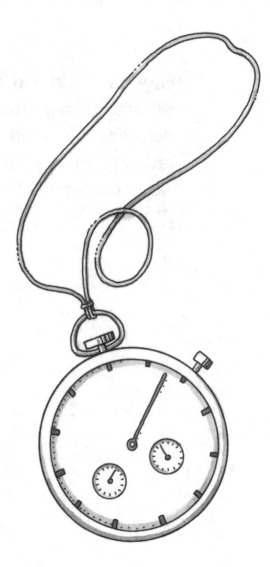

butterfly

heart

star

leaf

fish

ball

flower

Word Wall Storytelling

> Help children integrate individual words into a meaningful context.

1 Remove words from the Word Wall, one for each child. Give each child a different word card, keeping one for yourself.

2 Have the group sit in a circle as you begin telling a story: Hold your word card so children can see it and incorporate your word into a story opening. The child on your left continues the story, including his or her word in the process.

3 Continue around the circle. Tape record your efforts and copy the story onto paper, then reproduce so each child has a copy to read. Children can underline the Word Wall words in the story.

Variation

Challenge pairs of children to work together to tell short stories involving as many Word Wall words as possible. If your Word Wall has removable word cards, have children remove the words and arrange them in the order in which they appear in the story.

20 Questions

1 Choose one word from the Word Wall.

2 Direct children's attention to the Word Wall and have them take turns asking yes or no questions about the word. As they eliminate words, children can remove them or cover them with sticky notes.

3 The child who guesses correctly can be the next one to select the secret word for classmates to guess.

Morning Mystery Message

> **Put your Word Wall to use at the beginning of each day by linking it to your morning message.**

 Use chart paper to write a message, substituting blank spaces for some of the words that appear on the Word Wall.

 After sharing the message together, have children scan the Word Wall to locate the words they need to place in the blanks to complete the message.

3 Have children take turns suggesting Word Wall words to place in the blank spaces, then write them directly onto the chart.

To correctly complete this Morning Message, children locate Word Wall words with the "alk" word family ending.

Good Morning!
Today is Monday,
September 14, 2001.
Today we are going
on our nature____.
When we get back,
we will ____ about
what we learned.
We will write our
discoveries on our
____ board. :) Ms.Gray

Words in a Flash

Isolate words with a flashlight for whole-class reading practice.

1 Darken your classroom and use a flashlight or laser pointer to highlight words you wish to review.

2 Invite children to take turns holding the light and reading a favorite word or two to the class, which then repeats each one. You might also use the light to point to a series of words you want the class to chant in unison.

illuminate

Teacher Tip

This technique works especially well with words of the same word-ending family, with rhyming words, or with similar-sounding, difficult-to-decode words, such as *when, where, what, why,* and *who.*

butterfly

heart

star

leaf

fish

ball

flower

Dictionary Word Wall

Expand vocabulary as children explore word definitions.

1 Have children choose challenging words from their independent reading to record and display on the Word Wall.

2 Have them record the word in writing, then read aloud one real and one made-up definition for each word they chose.

3 Let classmates vote on which definition is correct.

1. A Native American tribe from the Northeastern U.S.
2. A special seashell with purple inside.

Wampanoag

butterfly

heart

star

leaf

fish

ball

flower

Now You See It...

1 Before children arrive, remove or hide one word card from your Word Wall.

2 Have children use slips of paper to write their names and guesses about which word they believe is missing and place these papers in a basket or bag.

3 As children watch, draw papers from the container until you pick the right one. The child who guessed correctly replaces or reveals the missing word card on the Word Wall.

Teacher Tip

If you maintain more than one Word Wall, try moving a word from one Wall to another before school and have children guess which word was moved.

Word Wall Memory Game

> Similar to "Now You See It..." (page 86), this game develops visual memory.

1 Have children study the Word Wall for one minute and then close their eyes. With a sticky note or piece of construction paper and tape, cover one of the Word Wall words.

2 Have children open their eyes and try to name which word is covered. The children should each write a guess on a piece of paper, then reveal the hidden word.

3 Children can see if their guesses were correct and their spelling accurate.

butterfly

heart

star

leaf

fish

ball

flower

Double Trouble

1 If children can locate words with one phonemic element (such as a beginning letter or a particular word family ending), they are ready to play "Double Trouble." Offer them *two* phonemic elements to locate in a word. For example:

❋ "I am thinking of a word that begins with _____ and has the _____ chunk in it."

❋ "I am thinking of a word that begins with _____ and ends in the letter _____."

❋ "I am thinking of a word that begins with _____ and contains a short vowel _____ sound."

❋ "I am thinking of a word that has a long vowel sound and ends in the letter _____."

2 Children take turns guessing the word, pointing to it on the wall, and reading it aloud to the class.

Variation

Offer only one phonemic element at a time.

Poetry Word Wall

A word family Word Wall can easily double as a poetry writing center.

1 Review the groups of words on the wall and have each child pick a word family. The children then generate additional words belonging to that family.

2 Working alone or in pairs, children rely on their lists to help them craft rhyming poems.

Word Wall Detective

1. Choose one child to be a Word Detective and have her cover her eyes and turn away from the Word Wall.

2. Have a second child choose a word on the Word Wall, using a pointer to show the target word to the rest of the class.

3. The detective then asks "yes" or "no" questions in an attempt to discover the word, such as "Does the word begin with M?" or "Does the word end in /ing/?" The class responds "Yes" or "No" to each question.

4. After guessing correctly, the detective selects the next detective.

Secret Password

> **Children assimilate different features of a word.**

1 Give children a series of five clues to a word you've chosen from your Word Wall:

Clue 1: My secret word is on the Word Wall.

Clue 2: My secret word has _____ letters.

Clue 3: My secret word begins with the letter _____.

Clue 4: My secret word ends with the letter (or word family) _____.

Clue 5: My secret word could finish this sentence: _____

2 Have children write letters on their paper based on your clues.

3 Children guess the word you've described.

Pass the Cream

1. Spray shaving cream onto children's desk or tabletops (tape waxed paper or aluminum foil to the surface first for easy clean-up).

2. Have children spread their cream to create "writing surfaces." Dictate a series of Word Wall words for children to "write" in the shaving cream.

3. Children can look at the Word Wall or write the words from memory.

butterfly

heart

star

leaf

fish

ball

flower

Spelling & Word Pattern Activities

Use these fun games and
activities to help kids practice
and reinforce spelling patterns.

butterfly

heart

star

leaf

fish

ball

flower

Word Wall Word-O

1 To play "Word-O," have children write 16 Word Wall words in random squares on a BINGO grid (see page 95) and give them clues about each word, one at a time ("It means to laugh softly," "It begins with a vowel," and so on).

2 When the children find the word on their grid, they say it aloud and place a marker on that space.

3 When they have their board covered in a line across, down, or diagonally, they call WORD-O!

WORD-O!

stretch	three	thread	splint	splash
s⬤	thrill	s⬤	splendid	⬤
strike	throat	Free Space	⬤	splurge
street	throw	s⬤	sprinkle	⬤
throne	⬤	sprout	sprint	spray

		Free Space		

I Spy

1. Use your Word Wall to play "I Spy." You can focus children on a variety of word skills and concepts, including:

   ❃ rhyming words

   ❃ root words, prefixes, suffixes

   ❃ grammar (spelling, capitalization, usage)

   ❃ parts of speech (nouns, pronouns, verbs, adjectives, adverbs, prepositions, conjunctions, interjections)

   ❃ word definitions, synonyms, antonyms, and homophones

   ❃ phonetic features (consonants, long and short vowels, blends, digraphs, r-controlled vowels, silent-e words)

   ❃ word endings and spelling patterns

2. To invite children to search the Word Wall, say:

   I spy with my little eye,
   a word that _____.

3. Complete the last line with a clue to the word you are asking children to look for, such as:

   ❃ a word that is the *antonym* of sad.

   ❃ a word that *rhymes* with cat.

   ❃ a word that is a *synonym* for run.

   ❃ a word that is a *verb* beginning with the letter *t*.

   ❃ a word that can be *defined* as a small laugh.

Big Words

Children practice spelling as they rearrange letters.

1. Choose a long word from the Word Wall.

2. Have children use the letters in the word to form as many additional words as they can.

CONSTITUTION

on	sun	nut
no	sit	cot
not	it	
tons	son	
stun		

Variation

Ask children to use the letters in the big word to generate certain parts of speech, such as nouns, verbs, or adjectives.

butterfly

heart

star

leaf

fish

ball

flower

Sparkle Spelling Circle

Develop knowledge of spelling patterns.

 1 Have children stand in a circle, then say a Word Wall word. Have the child to your left repeat the word.

2 Have the next child say the first letter of the word, the next say the second letter, and so on, until children spell out the entire word. Have the next child repeat the word. The next child says, "Sparkle!" and the person next to him or her sits down.

3 Repeat the activity until one child is left standing (that child gets to choose the next word).

Red Marks the Vowels

Build awareness of vowels, consonants and spelling patterns.

 1 When making Word Wall word cards, use a red marker to print the vowels and a blue marker for the consonants.

 2 If a word contains a word family ending, use a green marker to draw a box around the letters spelling the word family ending.

ABC Order

Help children practice alphabetizing.

1. Randomly select several word cards from alphabetized columns of words on your Word Wall. Distribute these cards to pairs of children, who do not see the words during the selection.

2. Pairs work together to replace the words in alphabetical order.

Vowel Word Wall

Help children notice vowel usage.

1. Divide the group into five teams and assign each group one vowel.

2. Groups generate a list of Word Wall words that feature their vowel, and add as many more words with that vowel as they can think of.

3. A representative from each group lists their words on the board.

VOWEL WORD WALL				
a	**e**	**i**	**o**	**u**
apple	egg	ice	otter	up
ate	elephant	igloo	on	umbrella
ant	send	hit	off	huge
hat	pretend	bright	hot	hug
rake				

butterfly

heart

star

leaf

fish

ball

flower

Scrabble™ Spelling

Provide tactile spelling practice.

 Provide small groups of children with a supply of Scrabble™ tiles.

 Place the tiles facedown.

 Invite children to take turns choosing one tile at a time, (until they have up to 15) and use them to spell any of the words on the Word Wall.

butterfly

heart

star

leaf

fish

ball

flower

Snap-and-Clap

1 Have children use a kinesthetic "snap-and-clap" technique to spell out the letters in each word. Show children how they can snap for the vowels and clap for the consonants. For example, the word "bag" would be clap-snap-clap; the word "about" would be snap-clap-snap-snap-clap.

2 You can extend the activity by having children scan the Word Wall to locate words with specific snap-and-clap patterns you provide.

Chant-and-Move

Use choral reading to help children master Word Wall words.

1 Chant Word Wall words aloud together. To keep interest high, chant words using a variety of different speeds, volumes, or pitches.

2 Try spelling the words while performing rhythm and movement activities, such as clapping, stomping, hopping, jumping jacks, push-ups, skipping, and jogging in place.

Handwriting Practice

> **Pair handwriting practice with Word Wall mastery.**

 Provide children with writing practice sheets featuring words from the Word Wall. You might also prepare double sets of handwritten word wall cards: one set in print and one in cursive.

Each time you introduce new words to your Word Wall, invite children either to practice writing the words or match up the two different sets of word cards.

Learning Center Activities

Integrate Words Walls into your literacy centers.

butterfly

heart

star

leaf

fish

ball

flower

Tongue Twisters

Invite children to play with sounds.

1 Share some tongue twisters with your class. Look together at the words that make up common tongue twisters and discuss why these sets of words are tricky to pronounce together.

2 Invite children to use your class Word Wall cards to create their own tongue twisters. They can arrange the word cards until they find a combination they like.

3 Children may record and illustrate their tongue twisters for inclusion in a class book of tongue twisters.

Logo Learning

Build awareness of environmental print.

1 Make three sets of word cards based on environmental print (logos or print found on packaging, in magazines, in advertisements, and so on).

2 For the first set of cards, cut out each logo and laminate it onto an index card or sentence strip. For the second set, use a copy machine to produce black and white copies of these cards. Cut out and laminate each onto an index card or sentence strip. For the third set, simply use a marker to print the words onto cards or strips and laminate.

3 Challenge children to match up all three versions of the word cards.

Word Wall Hunt

 Each day, near your Word Wall, post a simple Word Wall "Go Seek" task card for children to read and complete. For example:

"List five words that have 3 letters."

"List all of the color words."

"List the words that begin with the letter ___."

 Have children jot their lists in small individual notebooks (stored in a bin near the Word Wall). At the end of each day, compare list results and preview the task they will be expected to complete the next morning.

Art Starts

Add a tactile element to your Word Wall Learning.

 Provide children with individual chalkboards and colored chalks, dry-erase boards and colored markers, or water color paints and brushes. (Glitter crayons and colored glues are fun, too.)

 Invite children to practice writing Word Walls in the different mediums.

Pocket Chart Sentence Center

Help children form sentences from individual words.

1. Place a pocket chart next to your Word Wall and put a card reading "Sentence Center" in the chart's top pocket.

2. Invite children to use the Word Wall word cards to "write sentences" in the chart's pockets. You might include cards printed with punctuation (periods, question marks, exclamation points and quotation marks) as well as individual upper case letter cards so children can punctuate their sentences.

3. Include words culled from the literature you are reading, so the children can use those words as well as the Word Wall words in sentences.

Word Wall Reporters

Provide independent reading and writing practice.

1. Provide children with clipboards.

2. Have them act as "roving reporters," writing down certain types of words (such as nouns, verbs, or adjectives) they can find around the room, especially from Word Walls.

Interactive
Word Walls

Get children as involved
as possible in Word Walls
with these strategies and
activities.

Word Wall Homework

> **Integrate Word Wall words into children's home experiences.**

1 Send a list of Word Wall words home with children.

2 Tell families to post the list where children do their homework, so children can "spell-check" while doing it.

Mini Take-Home Word Walls

> **Use file folders to bring Word Wall words into children's homes.**

1 Use a legal-size manila folder, divided into sections and labeled with the same headings as your classroom Word Wall.

2 Have children print each Word Wall word on the folder before bringing it home. Then, each time you add new words to your class Word Wall, send a word list home and ask parents to help children add them to their mini-Word Walls.

3 By year's end, children will each have a complete word resource to use over the summer and to take with them to the next grade.

Child-Designed Word Walls

Set up a child-generated Word Wall.

1 Encourage each child to create a Word Wall of the Week based on a topic of interest. Help children write cards for those words they wish to display. Children might use large pieces of posterboard.

2 Before taking the walls down, photograph each child's Word Wall and mount on a mini-poster along with a list of that child's words.

Children enjoy using posters of music icons or sports heroes to serve as backdrops for thematically-related words.

Tricky Words Collection

Invite children to read for new words.

1 Provide children with index cards for recording new words, especially tricky ones, then set aside "Show & Share Word Time."

2 Children introduce new words to the group by first holding up their card and asking if anyone in class can pronounce and define the words, then by telling the class what each word means and where it came from.

3 On the Word Wall, arrange the word cards according to word type (nouns, verbs, adjectives), by initial sounds, or alphabetically.

butterfly

heart

star

leaf

fish

ball

flower

Learning-in-a-Bag

Cull new vocabulary from literature experiences.

1 Choose vocabulary words from the stories children are reading and write them on index cards.

2 Pass the word cards out to children. Have children take turns using the words in a sentence, then work as a group to place the word cards on your Word Wall in alphabetical order.

Children as Teachers

Let children use your Word Wall to play "school."

1 Choose one child to be "teacher" while others play the roles of the students.

2 The "teacher" can point to each word with a pointer, and the class reads each one aloud.

Word Wall Cheerleaders

Teach children a chant to review Word Wall words.

1 Choose one child to be the "chairleader" and invite him or her to stand on a chair facing the rest of the group.

2 Hand the chairleader a word card he does not show to the group. That child then spells out the Word Wall word cheerleader style, and the class responds. For instance:

Chairleader: "Give me a B!" (Class: "B!)
Chairleader: "Give me an E!" (Class: "E!")
(and so on, with C, A, U, S, and E)
Chairleader: "What does that spell?" (Class: "Because!")

butterfly

heart

star

leaf

fish

ball

flower

Instead of "Said"

Expand vocabulary with a Word Wall devoted to a list of synonyms for one word.

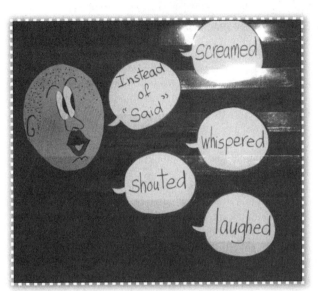

1 Post a sentence such as *The man <u>said</u> 'Go home!'* Point out the underlined word "said."

2 Then challenge children to generate a list of other more specific words to use instead of said, such as *shouted, yelled, blurted, whispered, mumbled, muttered, sneered,* and *joked.*

This pocket chart Word Wall uses dialogue balloon-shaped word cards to record synonyms for said.

Walking Word Walls

Increase the visibility of your Word Wall words!

1 Each morning, use a sticky note to print a Word of the Day.

2 Stick it onto your clothing so the children can see it and practice reading it all day long. You might try displaying the words in a different place on your clothing each day, such as the cuff of your pants or the elbow of your sweater.

3 Children can become Walking Word Walls, too, by choosing a word they want to wear all day long. At the end of each day, transfer the words to your Word Wall.

Spell Well Wall

Regard children's spelling errors as a chance to have children help you enlarge your Word Wall.

1 Each time a child does not know how a word is spelled or has misspelled a word, have him or her record it correctly on an index card.

2 Have the child add it to the Word Wall.

Test the Teacher

Let children give you a spelling test using words from your Word Wall!

1 As you face away from the wall while holding a clipboard and paper, have children take turns calling a word for you to spell on your paper. (You can purposely misspell some of the words.)

2 When each child has given you a word to spell, copy your paper so each child may correct your test!

3 You might also offer children Word Wall Spelling Tests in which all the spelling words come from the Word Wall, and children are allowed to peek at the Wall each time they take a test. This will delight children and give you valuable insight into which children have difficulty reading and copying from the Wall.